Run For Your

Life!

By

Cornelius A. Van Heest

For Mary Lou,

Jim, Wayne, Paul, Tom, and John...

"I consider my life worth nothing to me, if only I may finish the race and complete the task the Lord Jesus has given me — the task of testifying to the gospel of God's grace."

Acts 20:24

Table of Contents:

PREFACE:

"Run for your life!" That was the firm conclusion drawn for me by the heart specialist who delivered his diagnosis directly, "No one with any brains does to himself what you are doing!" My lifestyle was under attack; my intelligence was questioned; my future called into question! He was right and I knew it! The solution, for me, was to run in order to continue to live.

Running was not new to me; I had enjoyed four years as a varsity cross-country runner at Hope College decades before. I had even toyed with jogging occasionally—often enough to experience the pain and embarrassment of the occasional runner. But this was serious running... this running for your life.

Thus began a succession of years wherein running was an integral part of the weekly schedule, finding its way into the calendar book along with other significant appointments. Health improved; stress-induced chest pains disappeared; back pains caused by shifting discs no longer occurred; even cold germs were scared away! But the life I was running for was more than this.

The ancient Hebrews knew well that we are embodied spirits, so constructed that no segment of the person can be impacted without implications for the whole being. The apostle Paul, introduced to the world of athletics in his hometown Tarsus, clearly saw the picture:

"For physical training is of some value, but godliness has value for all things, holding promise for both the present life and the life to come" (1 Timothy 4:8). This book is an account of one man's rediscovery of this eternal truth. It is running for life!

I.   LIFE IS A RACE: RUN IT!

Often in the Bible, life is described as a race. But what kind of race best mirrors the race of life? Is it a brief burst of effort, a sprint soon ended? Is it a mile run which adds endurance to speed as requirements? Or is it a marathon, where speed is less important than dogged determination? Can it be an ultra-marathon of even 100 miles?

The answer to the above questions obviously is that God only knows how long our personal race of life will be. It has been my privilege through Senior Adult Ministry to run alongside real veterans in this race called life. In seeking to learn how to finish the race of life with grace, faith, and purpose, I have found these elderly saints an amazing resource—more helpful than the volumes on aging filling my bookshelves!

The apostle Paul in 2 Timothy 4:7 writes, "I have fought the good fight, I have finished the race, I have kept the faith." I have also been privileged to observe the crossing of the finish line by those whose race records 90 and even 100 or more years…faithful to the finish line!

In this chapter, I hope to portray the Christian life through the analogy of running as illustrations of the Biblical texts relating life to a race.

During my four years at Hope College, I enjoyed being on the cross country team. From where I ran in the races, the gifted runners were clearly in my view—ahead of me, all four miles! Perhaps, it is this running background which has made the Biblical use of running as an analogy so personally meaningful. My custom of jogging, still today, often is a time of spiritual encouragement as I experience aspects of running which mirror the Bible lessons for me.

Many persons who will be reading this book have already logged many miles. Senior adults are the veterans of the team. But we are still vital members of that team. Remember, rookies need the good examples of the veterans, and they are watching us more than we realize!

If life is like a race, what is its purpose? Listen to St. Paul's answer: "I consider my life worth nothing to me, if only I may finish the race and complete the task the Lord has given me—the task of testifying to the gospel of God's grace" (Acts 20:24).

"Testifying to the gospel of God's grace" is the race for the Christian. It's all about God's grace—not our goodness or our giftedness! Goodness and giftedness come from God; we don't create these characteristics— they are on loan for the race... of life. The life of the Christian is a Grace Race.

In the running of ultra-marathons—100 or more miles—the results of the race includes a listing of the runners and the time it took to finish. Often, there are names after which appear the letters DNF (Did Not Finish). In life's marathon there are no DNFs. The finish line for each person is set by God and every life is finished here—but the Christian's finish is really only the beginning! God looks for perseverance, not perfection.

Paul wrote to the Corinthians (2 Cor. 4:16-18): "Therefore we do not lose heart. Though outwardly we are wasting away, yet inwardly we are being renewed day by day. For our light and momentary troubles are achieving for us an eternal glory that far outweighs them all. So we fix our eyes not on what is seen, but on what is unseen. For what is seen is temporal, but what is unseen is eternal."

Runners who focus on their pain and fatigue or their place in the race are consuming energy and draining hope and therefore achieve less than they might have done. The inward (not the outward) and the unseen (not the seen) are to be the Christian's focus in this race of life.

In Hebrews 12:1, the writer paints an encouraging picture: "Therefore, since we are surrounded by so great a cloud of witnesses... let us run with perseverance the race that is set before us." Who are these witnesses he speaks of? Abel, Enoch, Noah, Abraham, Jacob, and Moses were cited as persons who lived by faith. But above all, the pioneer and perfecter of our faith... Jesus.

As a young teen-ager, I heard a noted RCA preacher deliver a moving sermon, "Saints in the Grandstands," based on this passage in Hebrews. I was moved by the thought of saints watching us run the Race of Life. Now, having passed my 80th birthday, I am more attracted to the thought of my looking at the lives of the saints than their watching me. And, in my mind, I have filled the gallery with a lot of other saints whose examples have blessed my life! From Sunday School teachers, to the only pastor I had from birth to college years—my dad—I have been abundantly blessed by examples of running the race of life! Teachers at Hope College and Western Seminary! Sisters and brother! Wife and sons! Members of the churches in which I was privileged to serve! My gallery is full and is still being filled!

Saints are those through whose lives the presence of God shines. They bless us when we see God as the shaper and sustainer of their lives. Sometimes, when we read of the lives of the saints in the Old and New Testaments, we seem to see only their great accomplishments. We see larger than life accomplishments. We need to read the rest of the story. For example, behind King David's amazing accomplishments in government and piety, there is the abyss of adultery and murder. The Hall of Fame, in truth,

—
8

is also a Hall of Shame. For David, shame preceded fame. He became a man after God's Heart.

Why examine the witnesses, then? Because for all the shame and fame, they didn't stay the same! They made excellence their passion. So can we! The crowd of witnesses is a pointer towards the Perfect One... Jesus. Runners are always looking to improve their personal best. The question we need to ask then is, "Are we whining or winning the battle for progress toward Christ-likeness?"

In the Hebrews 12 illustration, the runner being portrayed sees the crowd as a mist surrounding the track. Through the mist he searches for and finds the location where the emperor sits, surrounded by all the trappings of government. There is the face he seeks to please. There awaits him the reward for his performance in the race.

Let us look through the mists of the saints and seek the face of the Savior Himself... the One we wish to see and serve.

In my library of books on running, there are fascinating subjects: euphoria, hindrances, second wind, hitting the wall, team spirit, winning attitude, personal best, drifting, injuries, and etc. All of these subjects have equivalents in the Christian's life. The succeeding chapters will provide lessons for growing as Christians.

Our manual will be the Scriptures; our model will be the Savior. The Christians who make up our congregation, small group, class, or circle of friends, will be our team. We will seek to learn from and be led by Christ our Coach.

No matter the mileage of our race, the injuries we may sustain, the rigors of our training, or the ups and downs of the hills we meet, we will run with perseverance the race into which He has entered us. With the history of the saints behind us and the presence of our brothers and sisters in the faith before us, we will with perseverance,

—

run the race He has set before us!

QUESTIONS:

1. Does your Race of Life seem more like a challenge or a chore?

2. Whom do you see in the Gallery of Saints whose lives have modeled for you the Race of Life?

3. How well are you modeling the Race of Life for those around you?

II.   SECOND WIND

Runners claim that there is a point in the Fatigue Cycle where there is a sudden reversal called the second wind. Just when it seems the pounding heart will burst thru the rib cage, it suddenly paces itself as evenly as a pace maker. And as the lead-like legs threaten to collapse under the weight of the runner, muscles relax and rhythmically propel the body forward with ease! Lungs groping for air, now funnel oxygen effortlessly into the life stream of the runner; the runner has experienced the second wind! One writer explains it this way, "Something inside me felt as if it had just been connected to a set of jumper cables!" I would find this hard to believe if I had not experienced it myself—countless times!

More amazing than this is what the prophet Isaiah wrote in Isaiah 40:29.   A *spiritual* second wind awaits those who believe the promise and trust its laws. Trusting in the Lord provides an extensive exhilaration beyond the exhaustions of the spirit. "He gives strength to the weary and increases the power of the weak." Jesus explains it further, "Without me, you can do nothing!"(John 15:5).

Exertion leads to exhaustion; physically and spiritually, the principle is the same. Fatigue is a fact of life—at any age.

The age factor will introduce itself into situations of extreme exertion. Too soon, we discover that we can no longer do what once we did with ease. The process of aging is relentless. If this is true of the physical side of life, it is infinitely more true of the spiritual! The struggles of life take their toll. Discouragement and depression play no favorites. Doubt knocks on every door.

There is in Isaiah's message a realism: face reality! Life will tend to wear you out. There is, in yourself,

—

11

simply insufficient strength—physically or spiritually—to make it through. Before you reach collapse, admit that it is coming. Draw your strength from the only source which truly meets your need. Discover God's gift of a spiritual second wind!

By turning to God at each point of weakness and laying the situation before Him, we have access to this inexhaustible supply of power and strength. To experience the spiritual second wind is to be filled with the Holy Spirit so that all our energy and effort is coming from an outside source. We run without growing weary.

When we surrender control of our lives to God, it frees Him to let the second wind blow. This is not a denial of the talents or abilities He has given us, but it allows us to use them more significantly than we could ever do on our own.

The late James Fixx, author of two major books on running, was once traveling through a desert area near Phoenix when he saw a mountain beckoning him to climb. Exhausted, he reached the top where he met a gray-haired lady in tennis shoes. To his astonishment, she explained that she had been running up and down this mountain for years, every day but Sunday, often twice a day! But now, having reached 65 years of age, she had decided that once a day seemed enough. She had discovered that beyond exertion, there can be exhilaration. Mountain-top experiences were enjoyed daily!

In the athletic world of the runner, pressing thru exertion to exhilaration is an accepted reality. In the spiritual world, Isaiah urges us to hope in the Lord as we run our Race of Life and thus find, in Him, the source of renewal. Spiritually, we can find exhilaration beyond exhaustion.

It begins with faith… faith in God's promises. To

the distance runner the second wind comes naturally; to the spiritual runner, second wind comes supernaturally. In both cases, faith is the prerequisite. Believe it; try it; trust it; enjoy it!

Through exertion and exhaustion, to exhilaration, and to extension of the possibilities in our lives. When runners are asked to explain the concept of a second wind, they have great difficulty putting it into words:

- it's like running with wings;
- the heart, lungs, legs all function rhythmically, almost effortlessly;
- it is as though strength comes from a mysterious storehouse!

From somewhere it comes, unexplainably, but truly.

Spiritually, it is similar, says the ancient seer Isaiah. There comes to the *spiritual* athlete, strength to walk, strength to run, strength to soar! There will be fatigue and falling—even youths grow tired and weary. There will be times of stumbling and falling for youth and elderly and all the years in between.

Isaiah's encouragement is addressed to the weak and weary. Jim Ryan, once the world-record holder in the half mile and 1500 meters, trained himself to sprint when he was exhausted. His training method carried him to three Olympic Games! So, we too, can train ourselves to meet emotional and spiritual exhaustion by depending on God's strength in our times of testing. The challenge is to turn to God at each point of weakness, laying our situation before Him, and letting His inexhaustible supply of power and strength handle it for us.

Isaiah speaks of this second wind strength enabling us to walk, run, and soar. There are times when God lifts our spirits above the struggle to a spiritual mountain-top. These moments, admittedly, are few and far between.

Every mature Christian can relate several times when our needs were so great, our strengths so few, and our future so doubtful when God lifted us into His strong and loving arms and carried us.

An unknown author has written a beautiful picture of this soaring called ***Footprints in the Sand***:

> "I dreamed I was walking along the shore with the Lord, and across the sky flashed scenes from my life. For each scene, I noticed two sets of footprints in the sand; one belonged to me, the other to the Lord. When the last scene of my life flashed before me, I looked back at the footprints in the sand. I noticed that many times along the path of my life there was only one set of prints. I also noticed that it happened at the very lowest and saddest moments. I questioned the Lord about it. 'Lord, you said that once I decided to follow you, you would walk with me all the way. But I have noticed that during the most troublesome times in my life, there is only one set of footprints. I don't understand why in times when I needed you most, you would leave.' The Lord replied, 'My precious child, I would never leave you during the times of trials and suffering. When you see only one set of footprints, it was then that I carried you.'"

Yes, we can and do soar on wings like eagles. There is, in God's provisions, strength to soar. There is also strength to run.

A crisis arises, sometimes with little warning. All our energy is needed to get through the crisis. We need to draw from our past experiences; we need to aim at our hopes for the future; we need to make quick decisions and engage in demanding actions! Alone, we could not move this fast; we could not think this clearly; we could not walk so strong without the powerful presence of the Holy Spirit! He gives us strength to run!

Sometimes, in the ultra-marathon runs, the athlete finds it impossible to do more than walk. Patience and persistence become the priority and the necessity in our lives, as well. Isaiah claims that for those who hope in the Lord, they will, "walk and not be faint." Often, these quiet strolls with our Savior are the most life-changing periods.

In the life-story of every mature Christian, there is at least one season of struggle which remains forever engraved on our spirits—the powerful presence of our Living Lord! Through my eighty years of life, including fifty-four years of ministry, there have been several times when God has carried me through difficult situations: one, an automobile accident; another a series of three surgeries within six months.

One writer has written, "The promise of the Second Wind involves many of the great themes of the Gospel: hope, grace, forgiveness, and endurance, among others." In my moments of being carried, those themes became my sustaining force. May your remembrances of being carried in the past; give you assurance thru to the finish line when you fall into the arms of our Savior!

Questions:

1. What memories do you have of God giving you the strength to walk, run, or soar?

2. Have you shared these experiences with someone else to encourage them?

3. How have past experiences prepared you for what still remains in your Race of Life?

III. RUNNER'S HIGH

"Runner's High" is not as common an experience as "Second Wind." A Christian runner described it in this way, "My legs weren't heavy on the pavement; my lungs weren't desperate for air; my head was free from all distractions. My heart was beating with God's. I could feel Him breathing for me, though His air was my air. His strength became my strength, and when I came upon the wall too high to climb, He lifted me up."

Someone else simply said, "The only thing I can say about it is, I can't describe it." Still another person wrote, "We keep it to ourselves because we know no one could understand. How could they if we don't understand it ourselves?"

Looking back through past experiences as Christians, we find ourselves describing certain rare occasions as mountain-top experiences—as over against their opposite... valleys of despair.

In the Race of Life, most of us have run into a mountain-top kind of happening. It comes in the midst of a difficult struggle. And it comes at the most appropriate time! Many Christians call it "a God thing!"

Years ago, in the midst of an extremely challenging pastorate, I began to experience chest-pains. At first, I tried to ignore them. But the more I thought of my situation—a father of five sons and in my thirties—the more worry fed my pains! A visit to my doctor concluded that it might be early signs of a heart problem.

During one long night as I tried to sleep on a cot in the breezeway of our home while the weather recorded temperatures in the nineties, I wrestled with my worries. Suddenly, in the middle of the night, the room was filled with a white light—a silent presence! Immediately, I felt it

—

17

was the presence of the One I considered the Lord of my life! The light soon faded but it left me with a burden lifted! If He was there, what cause could there be for worry? Because He lived in my life, I could live! The deep valley was suddenly transformed into a mountain top!

The chest pains eventually were diagnosed as self-induced stress pains due to over-straining by over-working. The problem would occasionally reoccur, but the lesson learned has remained as a memorable mountain-top!

The tough times in life weigh us down into valleys of despair, but recognizing the powerful presence of our all-powerful Lord turns the valleys upside down into mountains of joy!

Since I was literally born at the base of the Catskill Mountains in New York State, I am very familiar with the view from the top. On a clear day you can see several other states in the distance. From our home, it was approximately four miles up to the top. It was a long hike, but very worthwhile. Down below, life could be a struggle, but on the mountaintop it looked awesome! Down below were chores, school, homework, and all of the tough times of growing up in a home with seven children in the years following the Depression. On the mountain top there was a resort area with two beautiful lakes and lovely beaches. In the valley was a garden which we spaded by hand and constantly weeded. Only later in life did I truly realize the beauty of the valleys. The little white church at the foot of the mountain and the little one-room school house a mile away are now happy memories. There I learned that God is there in the ups and downs of life. There I learned of a Heavenly Father who makes a heaven on earth thru His loving presence!

How would you like to take a short trip to heaven and then return with a different view of life? In his second letter to the Corinthians, the apostle Paul shares what it is like: "caught up to Paradise"… he heard "inexpressible things," things he was not permitted to tell. I am certain that his trip from the valleys of earth to the mountain-top of heaven was far more life-changing than my mountain-climbing youth.

On return, to keep conceit from corrupting his life, Paul was given a reminder which he termed "a thorn in the flesh." Whatever that thorn was, it wasn't pleasant. Three times he prayed for its removal. Three times he was denied. What was God's explanation? "My grace is sufficient for you, for my power is made perfect in weakness."

And how did Paul respond to all of this? "I will boast all the more gladly about my weaknesses, so that Christ's power may rest on me. That is why for Christ's sake I delight in weaknesses, in insults, in hardship, in persecutions, in difficulties. For when I am weak, then I am strong." He had been to the mountain-top, but he also knew the valleys.

The footprints of our race of life show trips to mountains and to valleys, thru pleasantries and thru pain. Life is a long race; however many years it contains. In the valleys, like Paul, we experience weariness from weakness, injury from insults, hurts in hardships, pains in persecutions, and dreariness in difficulties.

Often God surprises us with a mountain top experience! I was privileged to observe one of my senior adult friends swept up into a runner's high. Knowing that she was an avid fan of the Detroit Pistons, several of the nurses asked her if she would like to celebrate her 103rd birthday by attending a pre-season game of the Pistons. As they expected, her response was a resounding, "Yes!"

With several nurses and some of her friends, she was

transported the roughly thirty miles to the game in a huge white limo! At half-time she was escorted to half-court in her wheelchair. There, before thousands of fans, she was introduced, and then her favorite player, Tayshaun Prince, walked across the floor carrying a jersey, sporting his number 22!

A few days later, on her birthday, I visited her— knowing what I would see. A slightly built 103 year old woman, sitting in her chair, wearing a jersey #22!

Mountain-top experiences come in many different varieties. I have been privileged to witness many spiritually dynamic mountain-top experiences. There is no greater joy than seeing the Holy Spirit transform human lives to God's glory. In Luke 10:17, we read of 72 of Jesus's disciples returning joyfully from what Jesus termed a "harvest" as they reported, "Lord, even the demons submit to us in your name." They had been to the mountain top!

After trudging thru the early part of her race for a mile and a half, a runner continued for an hour and a half when, as she described it, "All at once I felt a sudden glow from deep within my soul. All was well with the world. Whatever worries may have plagued me vanished suddenly and completely. Was this the runner's high I had read about and heard from others? I felt at peace with my surroundings. I felt a deep love for what God had provided me. He had given me the gift of running after all. On and on we ran, my God and I."

Much of life seems more like trudging than running; sometimes, it turns into troubles that feel like a valley of despair. Then, according to God's timetable, our spirits are suddenly lifted. It feels like we have been moved to the top of a mountain from which we begin to see life more clearly… and more as God sees it! We begin to understand the experience of the apostle Paul—God's grace is sufficient! Real power is "made perfect in weakness."

Runner's high is not an achievement; it's a gift! God's gift! It is not running anything. Nor running away from anything. It's simply running in the awareness of God's presence and provision. It is our running with someone... our Saviour! It is exuberant, extraordinary, and enjoyable. It is uncommanded, uncontrolled, and uncharted. It is simply soaring spiritually.

A little-sung hymn begins with these words:

"Far off I see the goal—O Saviour guide me; I feel my strength is small—Be Thou beside me; With vision ever clear, With love that conquers fear, And grace to persevere, O Lord provide me."

("Far off I See the Goal" by Robert Roberts)

An appropriate song in response to an experience of a runner's high might well be as follows:

"Great things He has taught us, great things He has done, and great our rejoicing through Jesus the Son; but purer and higher and greater will be, our wonder, our transport, when Jesus we see. Praise the Lord, praise the Lord, let the earth hear His voice! Praise the Lord, praise the Lord, let the people rejoice! O come to the Father thru Jesus the Son, and give Him the glory—great things He has done!"

("To God be the Glory" by Fanny Crosby)

Questions:

1. Have you experienced Runner's High?

2. How did it change your life?

3. Have you shared your story with others?

IV.   RUNNING SHOES

Not dancing shoes… not lounging slippers… not military sandals… but running shoes! The apostle Paul wrote in Ephesians 6:15, "Having shod your feet with the equipment of the gospel of peace." In the Christian life, then, it is the gospel of peace which gives stability and mobility to life!

Long ago John Calvin wrote: "In any warfare, ancient or modern, messengers who are swift of foot and soldiers who can stand firmly are needed." Yes, stability and mobility are prerequisites for our lives to be all that our Lord designed them to be, to run well the race He has laid out for us.

Abraham Lincoln's feet were the feet of an athlete. At 22, he weighed 180 pounds and was able to outrun, out lift, and outwrestle any man in his county. He is quoted as saying, "When my feet hurt, I can't think!" Yet, it is also said that the Great Emancipator did more or less what we all do when we have trouble with our feet… nothing!

What does the running shoe contribute to the runner? In *The Runner's Handbook*, Bob Glover and Jack Shepherd wrote, "A good running shoe protects the foot from the ground, supports the foot structure, and enables the body to move easily over the running surface. Shoes are for: protection, support, traction, cushioning from the ground, balance of foot deformities, and the accommodation of foot injuries."

Doesn't that sound like that—at whatever the cost—investment in correct footwear is absolutely essential for a runner to be successful in his or her goals? And for the Christian—even more vital in his or her life—is the Gospel of peace!

Years ago, when I ran cross country races at Hope

23

College, I witnessed a continuing argument between our coach and one of our runners. It was not about what kind of shoes to wear; it was about whether to wear shoes. Cross country, then, was a four mile race over very uneven terrain and rough surfaces—and sometimes, late in the season—over ice and snow! But Larry refused to wear shoes. He had a strong case since he was one of the best runners in the league. He made headlines, attracting many onlookers. Larry won his case and ran bare-footed. And we never found out whether he could improve his time wearing shoes.

Larry Fabunmi was not the first bare-footed runner to gain fame. Abebe Bikila, another Ethiopian runner, won a gold medal in the Olympics, running barefoot through the streets of Rome. I must admit—I have never tried it—but I am convinced that in distance running, and even more, in the Christian's race of life, shoes are God's provisions for stability and mobility.

Stability and mobility are the Christian's Firm Foundation. The hymn, ***How Firm a Foundation*** begins with the following exclamation:

"How firm a foundation, ye saints of the Lord, is laid for your faith in His excellent Word! What more can He say than to you He hath said, to you who for refuge to Jesus have fled?"

The hymn is a song about stability. Our foundation is laid by placing our faith in God's Word, not in man's, not in ours, nor in anyone else's!

It is that stability that provides peace for us in our race of life. Primarily, it is a peace of reconciliation or peace with God. Peace with God is the foundation for peace within ourselves, peace with others, and peace with God's creation. There can be no personal peace or interpersonal peace without peace with God as the foundation.

Until we have settled the issue of our relationship with Christ, we will not find a clear conscience or a peace with ourselves. And peace with ourselves is the first and necessary step toward peace with others. We live in a day when peace with creation is foremost for many people. But without a peace with ourselves and peace with others, it is not possible.

The runner may approach his run with an optimistic frame of mind, but if he tries to run with dancing shoes or lounging slippers or even military sandals, his optimism will quickly fade. Fred Lebow—famous runner and founder of the New York City Marathon—said, "Inside our shoes are two of the most abused parts of the human anatomy: our feet. They absorb the initial impact of running, and pass it upward to the ankles, knees, hips, back, neck, and head." What good running shoes do for these problems, the Gospel of Peace does for our more critical spiritual problems.

The second verse of "How Firm a Foundation" continues the thought:

"Fear not, I am with Thee; O be not dismayed,
For I am thy God, and will still give thee aid.
I'll strengthen thee, help thee and cause thee
to stand, upheld by my righteous, omnipotent hand."

The Gospel of peace gives the Christian a firm stance. The great UCLA coach, John Wooden, once said, "It is the little things I watch closely—socks and shoes."

—

Watching socks and shoes led to an amazing career as coach.

Some authorities explain that the designs of most running shoes emphasize either shock absorption—which provides mostly cushioning—or motion control—which provides stability. Both are essential, however.

Our Coach, Jesus, watches closely to see how firm our foundation of faith is rooted in Him, in order to give a spiritual stability for the tests in our races.

Keeping five sons in shoes—my wife and I discovered—was not easy. One of our sons had his heart set on a new pair of Adidas—the classiest and most expensive of that time. We reached an agreement; we would give him the amount other shoes cost if he would pay the rest. When the scent of newness had passed and the Adidas had lost both their attraction and traction, he continued to wear them… on and on. His brothers mocked the sight and smell, but they never fazed him.

The gospel of peace, however, never needs replacement. It gives stability to the Christian's life; it also provides mobility—a willingness to witness anywhere our run with God takes us. The apostle Paul is a clear example of this mobility; this willingness to witness wherever God leads. He wrote in Romans 1:14-15, "I am under obligation both to Greeks and to barbarians, both to the wise and to the foolish; so I am eager to preach the Gospel to you also who are in Rome."

A number of hymns remind us of our call to witness where He leads.

"He leadeth me, O blessed thought! O words with heavenly comfort fraught! What-e'er I do, where-e'er I be, Still 'tis God's hand that leadeth me…. His faithful follower I will be,

By His own hand He leadeth me."

("He Leadeth Me" by Joseph H. Gilmore)

Another hymn celebrates this mobility:

"Anywhere with Jesus I can safely go,
Anywhere He leads me in this world below.
Anywhere, anywhere! Fear I cannot know;
Anywhere with Jesus I can safely go!"

("Anywhere with Jesus" by Jessie Brown Pounds)

John Henry Jowett in his book, *The Whole Armor of God*, challenges us to walk down the following roads:

- Despondency and despair,
- Bondage of blindness,
- Ignorance and confusion.

Jesus met many who had lost all hope in their future. His presence restored hope and painted a picture of a better life for them in loving relationship with their Heavenly Father.

Whom do you know who needs you to step into their circumstances to present a clear picture of a loving Savior?

Saul of Tarsus, blinded thru his encounter with Christ Himself, needed Ananias to call upon God to restore his sight and open the doorway to faith in a future.

Whom do you know who needs someone to enlighten them about God's love and saving grace?

An angel of the Lord (Acts 8) sent Philip down a

27

desert road to meet an Ethiopian Eunuch, in service of the Queen, to help him to understand the prophecy of Isaiah about Jesus.

Whom do you know that is confused about faith and needs a friend to provide guidance?

God provides both the stability and mobility for His people to befriend and lead to faith persons who are struggling. What doorways of opportunity is He opening for you?

Habakkuk 3:19 tells us, "The sovereign God is my strength. He makes my feet like the feet of a deer. He enables me to go on the heights."

The Hymn, "Fight the Good Fight" by John S. B. Monsell summarizes all this with these words:

"Run the straight race thru God's good grace.
Lift up thine eyes and feel His face.
Life with its way before us lies
Christ is the path, and Christ is the prize."

Questions:

1. Have you found that peace with God that is the foundation of peace with others and with yourself?

2. Are you allowing that peace to give stability to your life?

3. Is that peace providing mobility for you in your spreading out of your witness?

V.   D. N. F. DID NOT FINISH!

An ultra-marathon is a very long race. A hundred miles or more! Usually, there are many runners listed in the reports of the race whose race is categorized as "Did Not Finish!" But is this a fair assessment of their effort? The runners began the race with different abilities, various training programs, and contrasting expectations.

If the rest of the story could be told, the most heroic efforts may be found among those who ran less than the full one hundred miles! Illnesses, injuries, or simple inexperience may account for the duration of their runs.

Similarly, the sum of years of a life lived does not accurately disclose the real value of that life! Far more information and insight is necessary for a fair evaluation.

The Bible tells the story of a young man named John Mark, whose first mission involvement ended in a D.N.F. Acts 13:13 records, "Then Paul and his companions set sail from Paphos and came to Perga in Pamphylia. John, however, left them and returned to Jerusalem." John Mark was a D.N.F.

Later, as recorded in Acts 15:36-41, Paul and Barnabas were led by God to return to visit the believers in each of the cities where they had witnessed. When Barnabas suggested that they take Mark, Paul was not willing to take a "deserter" along with them. The disagreement between Paul and Barnabas became so sharp that they parted company. Paul chose to take Silas and went his way strengthening the churches. Barnabas, however, took Mark with him and sailed for Cyprus.

What would have happened, do you think, if Barnabas had not responded the way he did? For one thing, the Bible would have been sixteen chapters shorter. There would have been no Gospel According to Mark!

Mark did not finish this race, but God had a plan for Mark's life. To unleash that ministry, God supplied the encourager whose name was Barnabas. God could turn a D.N.F. into a writer of one of the four Gospels! The response of Barnabas to a difficult situation opens the door for us... as Paul Harvey would say, "to know the rest of the story!"

Encouragers perform while others pretend! Encouragers see potential while others see only problems! Encouragers care more about people than prominence! Barnabas was an encourager!

David Jeremiah in his book *The Joy of Encouragement* draws a mental picture of a master artist picturing an isolated farmhouse, in the middle of a storm, creating in the viewer's mind a sense of loneliness. Suddenly, the Master Artist takes brush in hand, dipping into the choicest yellow color... and with one stroke of the brush, fills the window of the farmhouse with light. What had been a picture of darkness became a cheerful light in the window! Encouragement is "a cheerful light in the window of the soul!"

At least five times in the Bible (I Thess.4:18, 5:11, 5:14; Heb. 3:13 & 10:25) we are commanded to encourage one another. It is a marching order to be exercised over and over, like the old-time cars which needed to be jump-started from time to time by another car coming alongside.

A young boy quietly watched his grandfather who had retired from his fruit farm spend his days with flowers and shrubs, beautifying his yard and supplying flowers every Sunday for his church. The boy didn't say much. He simply watched his model and mentor and stowed away information and grew an interest.

Years later, living in a mobile home community, he began to transform its surroundings. Flowers, shrubs,

31

lawn, even a bubbling fountain! The final touch, a small inconspicuous sign, "Charlie's Way. Thank you, grandpa." And so did the mentoring of my father-in-law inspire the talents of his grandson!

Who are some of the people who mentored you by their encouragement to help make you who you are today? Who was like a Barnabas for you?

Barnabas the Benefactor appears in the 4th chapter of Acts. Barnabas was a friend indeed to a congregation in need! There, we read, that he owned an estate, which he sold, and laid at the feet of the apostles. Barnabas sacrificed so that the needy might have their needs met— encouragement seen as **consecration**. By contrast, one couple pretended to give all the price of land they had sold. Barnabas chose to perform, rather than pretend!

In Acts 9 we see him befriending a convert in need. "When Saul of Tarsus, now renamed Paul, tried to join the body of disciples in Jerusalem, who did not believe him a true convert, Barnabas took him by the hand and introduced him to the apostles." Barnabas risked his own reputation by serving as a bridge for a new convert! Barnabas the Bridge—encouragement seen as **commendation**.

In Acts 15, when Barnabas wanted to take Mark on a return tour, Paul would not hear of it. A sharp disagreement followed. So Barnabas took Mark and sailed for Cyprus—encouragement seen as **compassion**.

Encouragement of children, early in their Marathon Race is a tremendous opportunity. Cheerleaders for their Game of Life are a vital part of their upbringing. What would such cheerleading look like?

First, our focused attention. Their race is just beginning. They are forming habits carried along to the finish-line. Giving them our time and making them a

—

priority sends a powerful message, indelibly printed in their memory.

Second, give them individual attention. While much can be done in groups, some things need individual attention. By accepting and encouraging their unique personalities and traits, we undergird their growth toward their God-given design.

Third, look for the good instead of the bad—genuine appreciation. The "bad" must be dealt with, but they will grow by the ways we encourage.

Finally, physical affection. Communicating their importance in ways they can feel has a powerful effect, long-remembered!

Written encouragement has its own advantages. It is seen by the recipient as a deliberate reaching out to provide a positive lift. Putting into writing has a sense of definiteness—unmistakably positive. Sometimes our encouragement seems to be a round-about effort to help; written encouragement is direct. Many words of encouragement are soon forgotten, while a written note may be saved for years! Face to face is always best, but writing to a distant person, overcomes the distance factor. Written encouragement leaves a legacy that lasts!

A job description for encouragers—as modeled by Barnabas—would include:

- helping needy saints,
- endorsing an unwelcome convert,
- accepting alienated believers,
- enlisting promising teachers,
- nurturing a gifted successor,
- and salvaging a youthful deserter.

In John 16:7, the apostle quotes Jesus as saying, "It

is expedient for you that I go away: for if I go not away, the Comforter will not come to you; but if I depart I will send him to you." The Comforter (Holy Spirit) has come to fill us with His presence so that we may be encouragers.

Most of us struggle with unworthiness. It is not a question of how worthy we are but of how available we are for the indwelling presence of the Holy Spirit. We live with the fear of making mistakes. We have been using Barnabas as a model for encouragers, and it would be misleading if we did not acknowledge that Barnabas was not perfect.

In Galatians 2:13 we read, "Even Barnabas was carried away and played false like the rest. Drawing back from eating with Gentiles for fear of the Judaizers." Knowing what is right and doing what is right are very different challenges. Standing on our convictions when in public and doing so in private are also very different assignments.

Being the embodiment of encouragement is only possible thru the powerful presence of the Holy Spirit in our conversation and in our walk! The mutual encouragement of the Family of God enables us to complete our life's race.

By God's grace and with the support and encouragement of our church family, we can finish our race. No need for a DNF (did not finish) label. Like the apostle Paul in II Timothy 4:7-8, we can say, "I have fought the good fight. I have finished the race. I have kept the faith. Now there is in store for me the crown of righteousness, which the Lord, the righteous Judge will award to me on that day—and not only to me, but also to all who have longed for his appearing."

Questions:

1. Who have been encouragers in your life?

2. For whom are you now serving as an encourager?

3. Are you able to put memories of failures behind and, learning from them, to press on?

VI.   HITTING THE WALL

Elijah ran for his life and then he hit the wall. He asked God to let him die. Hitting the wall is a familiar expression to long distance runners. It's that point in a race where it feels like the runner can go no farther. The entire system wants to stop.

"It is enough, now, O Lord, take my life," Elijah prayed. It was a sudden mood change from high to low from mountain to valley.

Who is this man called Elijah the Tishbite?   An austere, solitary man from the rugged valley of Tishbite. Elijah from Nowheresville! It's like referring to this writer as Neil the Kiskatomite!   Kiskatom—the place of my birth—is a bend in the road at the bottom of the Catskill Mountains in New York State.

In Elijah's case, he became a famous figure as the Spirit of the Living God empowered him beyond explanation. Hitting the wall was not the end of his life… it only seemed that way to him at the time.

Elijah had come upon the scene suddenly with a pronouncement that there would be no more rain for three years. Deliberately, this claim was delivered in the face of Baal worshipers—Baal, the god of rain. King Ahab and Jezebel (the force behind the throne) asked, "Who is this troubler of Israel?"

Elijah proposed a challenge between the 450 prophets of Baal and himself—himself being the sole representative of Jehovah-God. Alternatingly, they called upon their supreme being: first, Baal; and then, Jehovah (1 Kings 18).   The drama ends with Baal's followers humiliated and destroyed, and Jehovah's representative, Elijah, victorious and exhausted!

As Ahab rode off to report to Jezebel, the 46th verse

———

reads, "The power of the Lord came upon Elijah and, tucking his cloak into his belt, he ran ahead of Ahab (who was in his chariot) all the way (17 miles) to Jezreel!"

Jezebel, the real force behind the King, threatened Elijah's life if he did not disappear. Then, we read, (1 Kings. 19:3) "Elijah was afraid and ran for his life to Beersheba in Judah... a day's journey into the desert." Who knows how many miles? In the race called Life we never know what lies before us.

It was then and there that Elijah hit the wall. "He came to a broom tree, sat down under it, and prayed that he might die!" (1Kings 19:4)

God understands our moods of discouragement and can lift our spirits again by His quiet words. The reasons for Elijah's low were apparent to God. His fear of Jezebel caused him to run for his life to escape her evil attacks. He began to compare himself to some of God's great saints who had run their races before he had run his. By contrast, he could not see himself able to survive the anger of Jezebel.

Running from his problem—he discovered—only served to bring on extreme fatigue. The journey he had embarked upon seemed too much for him. When he arrived at Beersheba, he left his servant behind and continued on alone. Isolation added to his struggle. He pressed.

Working in and through it all, of course, was Satan himself, seeking to destroy this man of God who had stood up so bravely and victoriously in the contest with Baal's prophets.

Hitting the wall is a common experience retained in the memories of senior adults. This is an experience they hesitate to relate until the listener has proven to be an understanding and trusted person. I remember vividly the story shared with me during one of my regular monthly visits.

The conversation began like many others, but her voice softened and she spoke slowly, "I don't often tell this story … when I was a young mother with several children, I contracted polio. One night the doctor described how critical my case had become... and carefully indicated that I was not likely to survive. That evening, as I lay in bed worrying about the future of our family, I wept for my children who might soon be without a mother."

Exhausted and discouraged, she fell asleep. As her story continued, her eyes brightened as she described a vision which had appeared to her. She understood it to be a view of heaven. She described it as the most beautiful sight she had ever seen or could ever imagine. The details, she explained, were indescribable. The vision was followed by a voice saying, "You will not die!" Then, a beautiful smile spread across her face. "And here I am today at age 95!" she said softly. Runners would certainly file her story under the caption, "Hitting the wall!"

Our life stories will all differ, but sooner or later, we experience this phenomenon called hitting the wall. What creates this experience? In the pressures of life, we sometimes cease thinking realistically or clearly. In our exhaustion, our perceptions become cloudy. We withdraw into our discouragement, ignoring strong relationships which could instill courage and hope.

Typically, and ironically, these occasions occur often in the backwash of exciting and powerful, positive experiences. We stumble from the mountain-top and fall into the valley of discouragement. Times of testing can both exhaust us physically and drain us emotionally.

Elijah's story is not an isolated experience reported in Scripture. For example, we can learn from the similarity of experience seen in the life of John the Baptist. While Elijah hit the wall in the desert, John the Baptist hit the wall in Herod's prison where he sent a message to Jesus asking, "Are you the one who should come or look we for another?" Both of these great leaders—one in the Old Testament, the other in the New Testament—hit the wall! Should we be surprised when it happens to us?

What is God's provision for his runners who hit the wall? God allowed Elijah a time of rest first. He delivered no sermon or rebuke. Then, God sent wind, earthquake, and fire. Eventually, God spoke to Elijah thru a still, small voice.

Hitting the wall always seems to be an isolating experience; we think we must go through it alone. But, actually, God's love is constant, tender, unwearied and even anticipative. He sees what we miss: the wall about to be hit! He has an Elisha willing to pick us up to continue our race of life.

Rest and food, meditation, a renewed encounter with God, a supportive, encouraging friend, a new sense of calling, and an awareness that there are many more believers around us than we realize... these are God's gifts to us as we recover from hitting the wall.

The word "Elijah" means "Jehovah is my strength." Faith made Elijah who he was. The source of Elijah's strength can be the source of our strength. It will be tested and in the end will prevail.

God's leading is often surprising! Don't waste effort trying to analyze it. The beginning days of recovery are often the hardest days; don't quit! God's promises often hinge on obedience; don't ignore your part. God's

—

promises are often amazing; don't linger in doubt.

Dee Groberg wrote a moving poem entitled "The Race" about a father watching his son in a race. I close with just the message of the poem's ending.

The son, leading near the end of the race, suddenly trips and falls. "Get up and win the race," his father urged. Rising and running with all his might, the boy slipped again! At his father's urging, once more he rose to race toward the finish line. But in his all-out effort to make up the distance behind the other runners, he fell a final time! One final effort to do his best, brought him to the finish line. He had heard the cheers for the winner, but was not prepared for "the greater cheer" from the crowd as he crossed the finish line. To his dad, he said, "I didn't do too well." In his dad's reply is the fitting theme for us whenever we "hit the wall."

"TO ME, YOU WON. YOU ROSE EACH TIME YOU FELL!"

Watching intently as you run your race of life, there is a Heavenly Father. Each time you hit the wall, He cheers you on! No matter how difficult your race or how many times you fall, hear His voice:

"To me, you are winning the race when you rise each time you fall."

QUESTIONS:

1. Can you remember a time when you hit the wall?

2. How did you experience God's healing presence?

3. Who became a strong encouragement for you, like an Elisha?

VII. STAYING IN SHAPE

Shape is a key word for runners:

- "What kind of shape are you in?"
- "I need to maintain my exercise program to stay in shape."
- "I am getting in shape for a marathon."

What does it mean to stay in shape? Students of running are well aware that muscle strength and speed are not the same at age 55 as it was at 33; therefore, races are broken into age-group competitions.

The last two running events I participated in at Hope College I came home with first-place ribbons! There are two explanations I need to make: first, I ran in the category of 70 year olds and older; and second, I was the only entry in that age bracket!

In *Running Past 50* Richard Benyo writes about performance through the years. "Familiarity breeds contempt. Anyone who's ever teetered on the edge of a rut, or who's slid down slippery slopes, knows just how accurate these words are. Anything we do on a regular basis, whether loving a mate, or stamp collecting, or photographing sunsets, needs constant attention and renewal if it is to remain fresh, and, by remaining fresh, maintain our devotion." What kind of shape are we in spiritually? Are we giving the needed attention and renewal to keep our faith fresh?

Above all the characters we encounter in the Bible, the one who stands out for me as staying in shape is the man called Caleb. Caleb was captured by a vision of a Promised Land. While others faltered and fell, he remained strong—he stayed in shape!

42

What was his secret? Two phrases recur in his life story: "the Lord helping me" and "he followed the Lord whole-heartedly." Whether we peer into passages portraying his life in the 20s, 40s, or at 85, we find him pursuing a vision. He understood follow it or it fades!

I remember listening, with deep appreciation, to an 85 yr. old preacher speaking about his favorite subject: the ascension of Christ. I knew that he was "legally blind", but he looked at his Bible intently as he recited the passage from memory. His sermon manuscript was laid out on the pulpit and he shuffled the pages as he moved thru his sermon. Dedicated to his vision, till he died at 92 years, was my dad. These two lives, Caleb's and my dad's, continue to challenge me to remain expectant, eager, and enthusiastic to the end!

At age 20, Caleb was captured by the vision of release from Egypt to Palestine, from slavery to freedom. A nation of slaves was set free to journey to the land of their dreams—a land God had promised them! He was thrilled at the idea of starting life anew! His excitement grew as he saw God over-power the Egyptians, stop the Red Sea, and provide for a long journey for a great horde of people. Wholeheartedly, he followed God.

God releases His people, today, from bondage to sin into the prospect of living the spiritually abundant life— now and eternally! By faith, God opens our eyes to our future in our Promised Land. God's call regarding this heavenly vision is follow it or it fades!

Caleb, at age forty, was chosen as one of twelve men to scout the Promised Land. Joshua and Caleb were the only two among the twelve that brought back a positive report. The doubting ten reported a tribe of giants living in a mountainous region, and feeling like grasshoppers in their presence. Joshua and Caleb spoke of divine power to

—

43

deliver what He had promised. They refused to accept the grasshopper-theology; they clung to the vision. It did not fade, and they were ready to follow!

Their commitment reminds me of the hymn "O Jesus, I Have Promised" (John E. Bode):

"O Jesus, I have promised to serve Thee to the end; be Thou forever near me, my Master and my friend. I shall not fear the battle, if Thou art by my side; nor wander from the pathway, if Thou wilt be my guide."

The ten saw only difficulties; Joshua and Caleb saw the Divine. The journey to the Promised Land was delayed and a whole generation missed the journey! Throughout all those years of waiting, Caleb had stayed in shape.

Fred Lebow, the running guru, speaks of the need, as we age, of three things: acceptance, accommodation, and adjustment. While Caleb was waiting for the journey—from years 40 to 85—he *accepted* the reality of his aging, *accommodated* his lifestyle, and *adjusted* to the challenge of pursuing, at last, his vision! Caleb stayed in shape!

Listen to his words: "I am still as strong today as the day Moses sent me out; I'm just as vigorous to go out to battle now as I was then." Was this idle boasting? The record relates that Caleb led an army into the hill country, where the giants lived, and claimed his vision. The vision, which had seemed to vanish, emerged victorious!

In my ministry, I am humbled by the vision clung to by senior adults who have reached their 100th year. Patiently, their hearts have prepared for the final battle, they are following the Lord whole-heartedly, they expect

—

their Lord to come for them, they are eager to reach their heavenly home, they are enthusiastic about the journey, and they emerge victorious in their Promised Land! Spiritually, they have stayed in shape. They run the race of life well!

Years ago, we thought that a marathon, slightly over 26 miles, was a long race. Now, ultra-marathons of 100 miles are becoming more common. When I began my ministry, over 50 years ago, I never visited a person 100 years old. Now, I visit a number of them every month. And, spiritually, they are staying in shape.

Recently, I went to visit a senior adult who had just reached her 100th year marker. She wasn't in her room! After visiting a few others, I returned to her room. An activity offered the residents had captured her interest. When I found her home, she was busy crocheting a covering for hangers. Her eyesight is failing, so she works under a special light ... used most often in her reading of the Bible. When I left, she sent me home with one of her hangers—for my wife. Scripture reading, prayer, and crocheting keep her running her race in good shape! The Lord helping her, she stays in shape.

She reminds me of that hymn again, "O let me hear Thee speaking, in accents clear and still, above the storms of passion, the murmurs of self-will! O speak to reassure me, to hasten or control! O speak, and make me listen, Thou Guardian of my soul!" (O Jesus, I have promised)

Obviously, staying in shape does not mean maintaining the same physique of our youth. Nor does it mean reaching our 100th year looking like we're still in our fifties. It does mean that we are still growing spiritually strong because the Lord is helping us to follow Him whole-heartedly. It means that we are still expectant, eager, and enthusiastic and intend to be so through the tape. Finishing strong!

Caleb's vision, which had seemed to vanish, emerged victorious. Patiently, he pursued. Our physical eyesight may fade, but we can still see the vision! Our hearing may fade, but we can still hear the still, small voice! We may need walkers, wheel-chairs, and etc., but we can still march to Jerusalem!

We can still sing: "O Jesus, Thou hast promised to all who follow Thee that where Thou art in glory—there shall Thy servant be! And Jesus, I have promised to serve Thee till the end; O give me grace to follow, my Master and my Friend!"

Questions:

1. Are you at least as strong now, spiritually, as you were in your fifties?

2. What are you doing to keep your faith "fresh"?

3. Are you accepting the reality of aging, accommodating your lifestyle, adjusting to new challenges, and staying in shape?

VIII. FEAR OF FAILURE

A few years ago, in preparation for a sermon on this subject, I read three books by three different authors: Steve Farrar, Charles Swindoll, and John Maxwell. The title of Maxwell's book, *Failing Forward*, caught my attention. Normally, we think of failure as shoving us backward or at least slowing us down. The concept of failure as potentially being a forward moving experience was intriguing. Charles Swindoll's book, *Moses*, placed the concept of "failing forward" in a Biblical perspective. Steve Farrar's book, *Finishing Strong*, portrayed the same concept in the image of athletics, again picturing it in the life of Moses.

When Moses is placed in the Hebrew Hall of Fame in Hebrews 11, it is as a champion among champions. But the rest of his story tells of an up-and-down race. Moses' life can be divided into three forty-year periods:

- First, an unqualified success in Egypt where he was a somebody.
- The second period shows Moses as an undisputed failure in the desert.
- Finally, he appears fitted for the Master's use—God using a nobody.

Our race of life may not be so neatly divided into segments, but we certainly experience both failures and successes. But God's presence in our lives can change failures into successes.

Often, we try to bury our failures with excuses. Maxwell caricatures our "lame excuses" for traveling on "failure freeway" in an interesting way with imaginary excuses for driving accidents:

- "An invisible car came out of nowhere, struck my car, and vanished!"
- Or, "the indirect cause of this accident was a little guy in a small car with a big mouth!"
- A final entry, "I had been driving my car for four years when I fell asleep at the wheel and had an accident."

As long as we try to cover our fear of failures with excuses or denials, our Race of Life will not achieve the quality our Savior desires for us.

Swindoll describes Moses' journey—and ours—as having three flaws:

- We run before we are sent.
- We retreat after we have failed.
- We resist when we are called.

That's the sequence Moses followed. Does it sound familiar? Not waiting for God to arrange our future, we sprint ahead to make it happen.

It didn't work for Moses, and it won't work for us! The critical fault was, "He looked this way and that way… but not up! Moses became a 'frightened fugitive' … a failure!"

Swindoll's conclusion? "When God is in it… it flows. When He isn't… it's forced." Self-assumed actions do not have the same results as God-appointed actions.

Years ago, there was a race to be the first to fly. Dr. Samuel Langley was blessed with fame, funding, and facilities. By comparison, Orville and Wilbur Wright were uneducated and un-funded. It seemed an uneven contest. The least likely, however, became the first to fly.

Ultimately, Langley became demoralized and defeated. He gave up. Amazingly, just days later, Orville and Wilbur flew their plane, Flyer 1.

Winston Churchill once said, "Success is moving from one failure to another with no loss of enthusiasm." How true! How challenging!

Moses' initial effort to solve the plight of his people was ill-planned and ill-timed. Moses plan failed. But God had a plan—and it called for Moses to play a major role. But when God came to Moses in his desert dwelling, Moses could only mouth excuses.

Swindoll pictures Moses' excuses as follows:

- "I don't have all the answers.
- "I may not have their respect."
- "I'm slow in my expressions."
- And, "I'm not as qualified as others."

Unfortunately, enlistment in kingdom work too often today is still met with the same type of responses.

The challenge of the Scriptures is "Trust in the Lord with all your heart and do not lean on your own understanding. In all your ways acknowledge Him, and He will make your paths straight" (Proverbs 3:5-6).

Recently, our church had a dinner for its members involved in care for shut-ins and for those home-bound who were able to come to the dinner. I wondered who, if any, of our homebound would be able to attend. When I arrived, I was totally surprised by one in attendance: after countless months and multiple surgeries and still being fed thru a tube (as far as I knew), there she sat using silverware to feed herself! With amazingly strong faith, she runs her race. Not leaning on her own or her doctor's understanding alone, but acknowledging her Lord's will

---

49

and way, she is thankful for what she can do, rather than bemoaning what she cannot do!

In I John 5:4, we read, "For this is the victory that overcomes the world, even our faith." In the words of John H. Yates, "Faith is the victory! Faith is the victory! O glorious victory that overcomes the world."

Faith makes the Christian a winner in the race of life. Faith overcomes fear—even fear of failure!

The Race of Life is a struggle for confidence. I remember well my struggle for confidence, especially when I arrived at Hope College—just short of my 16th birthday. The old army barracks where I roomed for my first year at Hope housed sixteen students—a number of whom were returning veterans, all notably older than I. A number of them, including the veterans, decided to try out for the cross-country team.

Trying to cover my feelings of insecurity, I would make comments like, "Are all four miles run without any real hills? Back home, in the Catskill Mountains, we ran up and down *real* hills!" On the day of tryouts, they dared me to show them how easy it was to run the course. The conversations, for me, were never about running, but about self-confidence. Fortunately, I discovered that day that God had given me the ability to compete in distance running. I finished ahead of all of my "friends" though I could barely walk the next morning! My false confidence was born of a lack of confidence which God, in a strange way, began to change.

Moses moved from a false confidence, through a lack of confidence, to confidence in God. He had tried acting on his own, then experienced the paralysis of fear, and finally became a man of great faith.

How many times have we not been through the same cycle: "I can do anything by myself." Followed by, "I

—

can't do anything!" Finally, "I can do anything when God calls and enables!"

When Moses was wandering in the wilderness, he felt like an absolute failure. He seemed to have lost everything: career, status, reputation, family, friends, and a future. But he became certain that God was speaking to him; he became confident that God was all-powerful. In that confidence, he became comfortable with God's plan.

"Failing Forward" requires that we take responsibility for our actions, rather than trying to deflect responsibility toward someone else. It means learning from past failures in order to avoid repetition. Understanding that failure can be a part of a process leading to a more positive attitude, our race of life can find more solid footing. Refusing to think of ourselves as failures can lead to better choices. Choosing perseverance over quitting can bring about successes rather than failures.

The contemporary Bible translation called *The Message* tells the story of the turning point in Moses' life with these words: "The angel of the Lord appeared to him in flames of fire blazing out of the middle of a bush. The bush was blazing but it didn't burn up." There followed a conversation between Moses and God, while Moses hid his face, afraid to look at God.

God challenged Moses: "I'm sending you to Pharaoh to bring my people, the people of Israel, out of Egypt." Was there ever a greater challenge given to mortal man? What did God see in Moses that could possibly accomplish such a task? God saw in Moses a person who surrendered to God, and who could accomplish miracles!

As we come through times of failure, our forgiving Heavenly Father calls us to move forward in our lives of servanthood, acknowledging that God is very good at picking up the pieces of our failures and causing them to become times of spiritual growth which create the humility that qualifies us for successful discipleship.

What the devil determined to make a dead end, God makes a leap forward! The choice is ours. We can limp along—wounded by failures—or we can leap ahead with the powerful presence of the Living God, forgiving and empowering and guiding!

Questions:

1. Can you recall a time when, with humility, you sought God's forgiveness for your failure and felt the warmth of His love?

2. Have you ever shared such an incident with someone who was mired in the mud of failure and guilt?

3. Whom do you know who needs to know about God's forgiving, restoring grace?

IX.   FINISH STRONG

"Finishing strong" means coming to the end of your life in a strong relationship with the Lord Jesus Christ. Dr. John Gilmore, in his book **Ambushed at Sunset**, writes about coping with mature adult temptations. His list describes the flaws that can undermine our prayerful desire for a strong finish to the Race of Life.

Satan tempts us to, "withdraw, to be bossy, indifferent, gullible, to live in the past, fantasize, complain, to be bull-headed, to self-pity, worry, despair, suicide, put off." Gilmore's book attacks the myth that adults are not easily tempted.

Beginning runners and veterans are all tempted from start to finish in their races. All Christians are tempted throughout their Race of Life, and the Bible gives us many examples of a variety of finishes.

Steve Farrar, in his book, **Finishing Strong**, describes four types of finishes found in the Bible:

- Cut off Early
- Finished Poorly
- Finished So-so
- Finished Well

Samson in the Old Testament and John the Baptist in the New Testament were cut off early. Saul and Solomon, in the Old Testament, finished poorly. David and Hezekiah, in the Old Testament, finished so-so. In the category of finished well, Farrar lists Elijah, Caleb, and Paul.

Beginning a race well is one thing; finishing it well is another. I remember well my college cross-country running days. I always wanted to have a fast finish, so I

—

sprinted the last 100 yards of the four mile race. Now, as I look back, I wondered how slow I must have set the pace along the way to have had anything left at the end. Beyond the finish line tape, I quickly disappeared to experience what we called dry heaves! I knew so little about running. I had a psychology professor and, later, a sociology professor as coaches. I learned a lot about those two subjects, but little about running. Mainly, because I didn't listen too well!

Runners in the Race of Life might well sing Frances Havergal's hymn, "Like a River Glorious":

"Trusting in Jehovah, hearts are fully blest; finding as He promised—perfect peace and rest."

Farrar, in his book, wrote: "Those who are stayed upon Jehovah" consistently do four things:

- Stay in the race,
- Stay close to Christ and Christians,
- Stay away from evil,
- And Stay alert for temptations.

We can't finish strong if we don't stay in the race! Aging causes us to do many things differently because physically or mentally we have different capacities than earlier. God understands and expects us to make adjustments as we proceed in the race of life, but He calls us to stay in the race thru the finish line.

We, alone, can run the race, but we don't have to run it alone. I enjoyed running cross-country because cross-country is a team sport. There is a coach, and there are runners. Christianity is a team sport. There is a coach

(Jesus), and there is a team (the Christian Church). Teammates encourage each other to finish strong by staying in the race.

The Race of Life is finished best when the runners stay close. The strongest effect on our race of life is our relationship with Christ because we truly run in His strength. Finishing strong can only be credited to the presence of Christ in our lives… our running.

The Race of Life is also run best when the runners (Christians) stay close to each other. Two of Satan's most common lies are you don't need the church and you don't need other Christians in your life.

Four miles, I found out, is a long way to run alone. Life is a long race to run alone. I also am discovering that the ultra-marathon—often over 100 years—needs *even more* the strong presence of fellow-Christians and the Christian church.

The Race of Life cannot be run well if we do not stay away from evil. The strongest opponent in the race of life is Satan. Coaches are well-known for their "rules" for their athletes. The quality of the race run is often determined by activities engaged in by the athlete between races. The training rules if followed, enhance the race; if broken, they inhibit the quality of the race. Satan has not stopped his whispering since he corrupted Adam and Eve!

Staying away doesn't happen by chance. It requires staying alert. Satan is subtle. Friends often mock the discipline of the athlete, like Satan who whispered in the Garden. It is true that we don't get to heaven based on our perfect life-style, but by grace alone. But doesn't "grace received" require "gratitude expressed" in how we run our race?

The Bible is filled with word pictures of senior saints. In the second chapter of Luke's Gospel, Simeon and Anna model for us how to run the closing miles of the race of life.

Simeon and Anna finished their race of life spiritually strong. In difficult days, they clung to the promise of God that He would send a redeemer to save His people. While others had either forgotten, rejected, or perverted the promise, they held that hope strongly in their hearts. Simeon and Anna were strong finishers!

The setting for their strong finish was what the Jews called a "Presentation." Joseph and Mary took Jesus to the Temple to offer a sacrifice. In their case it was a pair of doves or two young pigeons—an offering the poor would bring, in place of a lamb. Joseph and Mary were not wealthy. They were ordinary people chosen for an extraordinary purpose!

Where the news went was not subject in those days to the bias of the media, but to the choice of God. Simple shepherds received the first signal of the good news. Distant Wisemen heard by way of a star. Simeon and Anna were drawn by the quiet inspiration of the Holy Spirit of God. Open to the Spirit of God, they heard the news clearly: God is about ready to fulfill His promise! Their lives became directed by God. Inspired, revealed, directed... they were ready!

Simeon and Anna spent their lives driven by the desire to know the Messiah... not to know about Him, but to know Him. When Simeon saw the baby Jesus and held Him in his arms, he turned to God and said, "I'm ready to go in peace. I have seen the Messiah." Anna, too, spent her days in the Temple courts waiting for what would make all those long hours eternally worthwhile... the chance to see the Messiah who would redeem her people!

The Race of Life for the Christian finishes strong when we see Jesus. When we worship Him face to face!

What would God have our conversations sound like as we approach the finish line? Should it be filled with degenerative words, such as, downhill, decline, disease, dependency, depression, decrepitude? Or regenerative words, like, renewal, rebirth, revitalization, rejuvenation, and resurrection?

I remember well a cross country race in which we knew the score would be close. From the start of the race I increased my pace. It all seemed to go well until I was a quarter mile from the finish line. I began to doubt if I could even finish.

Then, suddenly, I noticed, running alongside me, my friend who was the top runner in the league. I wondered what he was doing so far back in the pack. Then I realized, he had already finished, winning the race, and returned a quarter of a mile to run alongside me... to encourage me!

I thought that was really nice until he spoke, "Pass that fellow ahead of you!" I was going to explain to him how tired I was, and then I realized I couldn't say that to him. I mustered what energy was left and passed the runner he had indicated.

He spoke again, "Pass the next runner!" Again, I could find no way to excuse myself from digging a little deeper and passing one more runner. When we had repeated the procedure one more time, I reached the finish line.

Then, with amazement, I realized what he had done. After finishing and winning the race, he had come back to encourage and inspire me to finish better than I believed possible!

Finishing the Race of Life is made possible and is greatly enhanced by the Saviour who has run the race of life on earth perfectly and now desires to run alongside us, so that we can finish strong and enjoy life eternal with Him!

QUESTIONS:

1. Simeon lived for the fulfillment of a promise. What promise do you long to be fulfilled by God?

2. Anna would spend all day and night in the Temple—how would God have you spend your retirement years?

3. It is written of Simeon that, "The Holy Spirit was upon him." How do you sense the Holy Spirit in your life?

X. ILLNESS AND INJURY INTERRUPTIONS

Illness and injury, what do they interrupt? They interrupt our responses to the opportunities for service which God so graciously sets before us. He has created each one of us for a purpose. Illness and injury, however, can block us from fulfilling those purposes. But it is the same God who opens up opportunities that allows the interruptions. Our race of life is planned in advance and His design allows for both.

Injuries and illnesses sure can change schedules. They also test our patience. And yet, they have the potential for teaching vital lessons.

Some years ago I visited the indoor track facility at Hope College. I noticed two things immediately: the track was sharply pitched around the corners and the rule was no changing directions on any given day. Without thinking, I jogged six miles. Because one knee was always on the low side, it carried the bulk of my weight. The knee on the low side rebelled and tore a cartilage! Surgery addressed the situation but left its mark. We often ask the question, "Why do injuries happen?" In this case, the answer was obvious: guilty as charged!

Looking back over the years, I am sure many of us could identify self-imposed injuries and illnesses as well. The number one reason for injuries in running is overuse— running too fast, too soon, or too often. Is it any different in the race of life? Overloading our schedules, living too fast in order to keep up with our schedules, jumping back into workloads too soon after illnesses, and ignoring warning signs too often can open the door to injury or illness.

John Peterson's hymn, "So Send I You," pictures God's call to our lives:

"So send I you My strength to know in weakness, My joy in grief, My perfect peace in pain, to prove My power, My grace, My promised presence. So send I you, eternal fruit to gain. As the Father hath sent Me, so send I you."

It is based on John 20:21, "Peace be unto you; as the Father hath sent me, even also send I you."

One of Charles Wesley's lesser known hymns, "Forth in Your Name I Go," concludes with these words:

"Gladly for you may I employ all that your generous grace has given and run my earthly course with joy and closely walk with you to heaven."

That certainly is the ideal goal!

An interesting story is told in Luke 4:38-39. "Jesus went to the home of Simon Peter. Peter's mother-in-law was ill with a high fever. Jesus spoke and the fever left her." Then, the passage relates, "She got up at once and began to wait on them." Gratitude for God's healing from sickness or injury, obviously, should express itself in serving Him by serving others. Should not our experiencing healing of injury or illness prompt in us a deep gratitude, expressing itself in service to others in His name? When injury or illness strikes our lives or the life of a loved one, our first thought is to lift our voices in prayer for God's healing. Should not our first response to answered prayer find expression in ministry to others?

Occasionally, God intervenes in the course of seemingly incurable diseases. Luke, a physician, logs the stories of many of Jesus's healings. In Luke 8:43, he tells

—

the story of a woman who had an issue of blood for twelve long years. Mark writes about the same woman, that she had suffered a great deal under the care of many doctors and had spent all she had. Yet, instead of getting better, she grew worse. In faith, she reached out and touched Jesus' garment and was healed! "Go in peace and be freed from your suffering," Jesus said.

According to the law of that time, the woman was considered "unclean" and, therefore, was restricted in her contact with others for those 12 years! I can only imagine how she must have spread the good news of Jesus wherever she traveled for the rest of her life!

One of the most important treatments for illness or injury is rest. Yet, it is, probably, one of the most ignored. Some years ago, I experienced what is called a hamstring muscle pull. The hamstring pull was significant enough to keep the fastest of runners, Steve Williams and Marty Liquori, from the 1976 Olympic Team. Yet, it didn't stop me from entering the 50 yard dash at a meet for Senior Adults some years ago in Grand Rapids. It didn't stop me from entering, but it did stop me from finishing. Twenty yards into the race, I pulled the hamstrings in both legs, simultaneously, and my face met the turf. Failure to find healing thru rest had its consequences, but provided a memory that cannot be forgotten.

God allows the interruptions of illness and injury for His purposes. They are to provide occasions for spiritual growth. Through these trying times we can discover the importance of adequate conditioning, the scheduling of warm-up and cool-down periods, proper life-style, and the importance of adequate equipment.

Preparation precedes participation. Worship, study of Scripture, prayer, and meditation prepare us for healthy discipleship. There is a time to stir our spirits and a time to

—

find the comfort of calmness. Learning the lessons of discipleship enables us to live as disciples. Seizing the opportunities for training in servanthood readies us to serve.

Since I have passed the three-quarters of a century mark in age, I have been noticing how our bodies begin to betray us! They become more brittle, less flexible, and gradually lose muscle strength. We become more susceptible to illness and injury. Sensing signs of fatigue and over-use and reacting properly will enable us to out-run and outlast those who go all out all the time.

These same concerns about physical strength apply also to our discipleship in the church. Over-commitment and over-involvement in church activities can lead to burn-outs and drop-outs. Similarly, an under-involvement can lead to spiritual anemia and fade outs. A careful study of the life of Jesus discloses how He, from time to time, ditched the disciples for quiet times alone with His Heavenly Father. His handling of His humanity can be an example to emulate.

In II Samuel 9, we read a fascinating story of Mephibosheth, son of Jonathan and grandson of Saul. King David asked: "Is there anyone still left of the house of Saul to whom I may show kindness for Jonathan's sake?" The answer was, "There is still a son of Jonathan who is crippled in both his feet." He had been given a name meaning, "shameful thing." Because of his unique relationship with Jonathan, David brought this unfortunate young man to a permanent place at the King's table.

There are still illnesses and injuries that leave a permanent mark with severe limitations that are lifelong. Such physical, emotional, or spiritual struggles are too often ignored. There was a place at King David's table for Mephibosheth. David acted with respect and love to make

—

an outsider an insider.

As servants of the King of Kings, we are under order to do all in our power to reach out to persons today who are living with such life-long struggles—physical, emotional, or spiritual—to provide space at His table thru grace-based ministries.

In the book, ***Running Injury Free***, Joe Ellis offers an outline for avoidance of injuries:

1. Find a friendly surface.
2. Warm up and cool down.
3. Stretch firmly but gently.
4. Keep your training schedule flexible.
5. Alternate *hard* and *easy* training.
6. Pace and space your race.
7. Keep records of your running.

Translated into Serving the Saviour Sensibly, it would read:

1. Form friendships within the faith.
2. Prepare and reflect on your performance.
3. Aim at gradual spiritual growth.
4. Be flexible in your scheduling.
5. Accept assignments both simple and challenging.
6. Control your calendar: pacing and spacing events.
7. Monitor your memories.

Blessed is the athlete who has a caring and gifted coach! Most coaches, at one time, were athletes themselves. Their abilities vary. The athlete's performance is strongly molded by his coach. Sometimes, it is not easy for the coach to find quality time for personal contact with the athlete. The duration of the coach-athlete relationship often is very brief. Great coaching is sought by developing athletes; sometimes without success.

In the case of every Christian, however, there is available a perfect coach: Jesus! The record of His own performance is one of perfection. His availability is constant. This Coach is with His athletes all the way to the finish line and beyond! So let us run our race, perfectly coached, with perseverance, confidence, courage, and great joy!

Questions:

1. What lessons have you learned from an injury or illness?

2. How has such a lesson helped you to run your race of life better?

3. How are you preparing to handle your next illness or injury better?

XI. RUN FOR THE PRIZE!

The race of life is a run for a prize. The apostle Paul wrote in 1 Corinthians 9:24, "Do you not know that in a race all the runners run, but only one gets the prize? Run in such a way as to get the prize!" Unlike races, as we know them, the Race of Life does not have only one winner. Therefore, the apostle urges us all to run so as to win. In Paul's letter to the Philippians, he offers his personal aim: "I press on toward the goal to win the prize for which God has called me heavenward in Christ Jesus."

The hymn writer, Howard Grose, wrote:

"Give of your best to the Master,
Give Him first place in your heart;
Give Him first place in your service,
Consecrate every part.
Give and to you shall be given;
God His beloved Son gave;
Gratefully seeking to serve Him,
Give Him the best that you have."

("Give of Your Best to the Master")

"Running for the prize" deserves the best physical, mental, and spiritual resources of which we are capable.

As I began this article, my mind drifted back to memories of prizes which I had won in past races. The only evidences of victory that remain had to be searched for to uncover! One is six inches high and reads: "First place 5K 1982. The other two are medals with red, white, and blue ribbons. Distant memories of long-forgotten races. The apostle was accurate: "The victor's crowns do not last!" He wrote, "They do it to get a crown that will

---

not last, but we do it for a crown that will last forever," (1 Corinthians 9:25).

By contrast then, the apostle directs our attention to the "crown that will last forever"... eternal life in the presence of our Savior and Coach, the Lord Jesus Christ!

When Paul wrote, "Run in such a way as to get the prize," many of his readers could easily visualize his message, since Corinth annually hosted what was called the Isthmian Games—similar to our Olympics. They would have observed the efforts of runners to win the crown of "laurel leaves"—a quickly fading testimony to a victory. How small a prize when compared to eternal life!

Running looking back over one's shoulders to see how someone else is doing is dangerous. Paul wrote in Philippians 3:13-14, "One thing I do: forgetting what lies behind and reaching forward to what lies ahead, I press on toward the goal for the prize of the upward call of God in Christ Jesus."

Ken Radke tells the story of a race focusing on Roger Bannister and John Landy in a race billed as The Dream Mile. They began the race a little slower than they had intended, checking out their main opponent. Bannister fell behind and Landy tried to keep an eye on where he was. While Landy looked over his left shoulder on the last lap, Bannister was beginning to pass him on the right. Before he could pick up speed again, he had lost the race to Bannister!

Looking back and dwelling on the past, or comparing ourselves with other runners can be discouraging. It also detracts attention from our future goals. Memories of past failures may become like weights slowing down our pace in the present and the future.

Running for the prize includes keeping in shape physically and intellectually as well as spiritually. In 1

Corinthians 9:24-26, Paul wrote, "Therefore, I do not run like a man running aimlessly. I do not fight like a man beating the air. No, I beat my body and make it my slave so that after I had preached to others, I myself will not be disqualified for the prize."

As our lives unfold, we discover, God has laid out for us surprising turns in our course to be run. Jim Ryan, one of our nation's greatest runners, tells this story, "For a lot of years I was pretty self-centered. I ran for myself. I knew God had given me the talent and the stamina, but I never actually ran for Him." After his running career was ended, this three-time Olympian opened Jim Ryan Running Camps where he could offer training tips and spiritual advice to young runners. "Running with Jesus", he explained, "has brought me the freedom and happiness that running for myself never could. This is worth more than an Olympic gold medal."

There is a danger here to be avoided! We are not to conclude from this athletic metaphor that using words like run, strive, press on, compete, or lay hold of suggest *works* which earn the prize! They are expressions denoting the faith that opens the door to God's gracious gift of eternal life. And it is God who gives us faith through the empowering presence of the Holy Spirit. The faith that perseveres is ultimately the gift of God—grace that grasps us and propels us forward!

The Bible is filled with warnings, admonitions, and exhortations; these are road-signs for the spiritual marathoner to build our confidence in the indwelling Holy Spirit and His ability to carry us along!

The process of aging has a strong impact on how we run. Recently, one of my homebound seniors—an inaccurate description—took me on a tour from the days of her very active and involved years as a secretary to her very active lifestyle living alone! Maintaining a strong interest in her church, her family, and her friends, she has burst the bonds of the home-bound and triumphed over the potential of being lost in loneliness. Feeding on Scripture, empowered thru prayer, she is a joy to visit and a source of great encouragement. She is still running well… from her easy chair!

The apostle Paul sums it up in Ephesians 2:8-10: "For it is by grace you have been saved through faith—and this not from yourselves, it is the gift of God—not by works, so that no one can boast. For we are God's workmanship, created in Christ Jesus to do good works, which God prepared in advance for us to do."

Good runners, usually, have great coaches who go out of their way to guide them. The success of the athlete is the joy of the coach. Behind them both is the creator God who graciously gifted each of them so that together they might achieve the prize of victory. Our Coach, Jesus, invests in us His guidance, encouragement, and example. The only perfect runner is the necessary part in our hope for heaven. Unless physically gifted, a runner cannot reach his goal: the prize. Unless the Savior's sacrifice is applied to our situation—there can be no prize of eternal life. Paul encouraged his young associate, Timothy, with these words: "Physical training is of some value, but godliness has value for all things, holding promise for the present life and the life to come," (1 Tim. 4:8).

We live in a world where great stress is being placed on physical training for a longer and more fulfilling life. In Paul's day there was similar stress on bodily training. While he did not discourage it, he contrasted its value when compared to "training for godliness." Physical training, he pointed out, has short-term benefits. Training in godliness, however, has more than long-term benefits.

—

Its benefits are eternal! The apostle does not dismiss the value of bodily training. He acknowledges its place and uses it as an image with spiritual significance.

The contrast he draws relates to the long-term benefits... the eternal life with God in heaven. The prize for which we compete is not a fading flower but an unending future in God's presence!

John Monsell wrote a familiar hymn, "Fight the Good Fight." The 2nd and 4th stanzas read:

"Run the straight race through God's good grace.
   Lift up thine eyes and seek His face.
Life with its way before us lies;
   Christ is the Path, and Christ the Prize.

Faint not nor fear, His arms are near.
   He changeth not and thou art dear,
Only believe and thou shalt see
   That Christ is all in all to thee."

"Run in such a way as to get the prize." Not drifting aimlessly from day to day. Not seeking ribbons, trophies, medals, plaques, fame or fortune. Not looking back at past failures. Not constantly comparing yourself with current champions. Not in competition with others, but in companionship with Christ!

Draw your game plan from God's Word. Follow in the footsteps of Christ your Coach. Know that your future is secure in your Lord. Rejoice in the privilege of living to His glory. Run from here to Eternity!

Questions:

1. Are you looking up instead of back?

2. What are you doing to keep in shape?

3. Are you listening carefully to your Coach?

XII. DRIFTING OFF COURSE

The writer to the Hebrews wrote: "We must pay more careful attention to what we have heard so that we do not drift away" (Hebrews 2:1). The apostle Paul wrote to the Corinthians, "I will run in such a way, as not without aim" (I Corinthians 9:26). Aiming attentively, therefore, is a major challenge.

Two runners of equal ability competed in a six mile race. In the last half mile, they each took a different route to the finish line. One of them had taken a wrong turn and his whole race was in vain. Drifting off course can be costly!

The apostle Paul observed that the Galatians had abandoned the gospel of faith by requiring certain good works. He wrote to them, "You were running well, what hindered you from obeying the truth?" (Galatians 5:7).

As we move into older adulthood, the highest risk is not open rebellion from our faithful following of Christ; rather, it is a quiet drifting from our faith walk. Neglect becomes a major temptation: neglecting the reading of Scripture, neglecting periods of prayer, neglecting fellowship with people of faith, neglecting opportunities to serve Christ in church and community. Drifting is dangerous. The simple truth is, "Be humble or stumble!"

The ship that is carelessly allowed to drift past a harbor because the mariner has forgotten to allow for the wind, the current, or the tide is a picture of this problem... the peril of a drifting life. The word used by the Greeks for the tying of a boat to a dock was "to moor a ship." The wise sailor does not simply say, "I tied the boat," but "I *secured* the craft."

The hymn, "My Anchor Holds" by William C. Martin, begins with these words:

—

"Though the angry surges roll on my tempest driven soul, I am peaceful, for I know, wildly though the winds may blow, I've an anchor safe and sure, that can ever more endure. My anchor holds!"

The Bible translation called **The Message** renders Galatians 3:3 with these words: "Let me put this question to you: How did your new life begin? Was it by working your head off to please God? Or was it by responding to God's message to you? Are you going to continue this craziness? For only crazy people think they could complete by their own efforts what was begun by God. If you weren't smart enough or strong enough to begin it, how do you suppose you could perfect it?"

God has a plan for each life. Constructing our own plan does not build on His foundation and will not withstand the storms of life. Often, we are not aware of our subtle change of plans—it is more drifting than deciding. The stagnancy of our routine causes a loss of focus. We tell ourselves, *It's just doing what I've always done! We did not mean to drift off course… it just happened!*

It's more like a daydream detour. We are not anchored to the Master's plan. At first, it is not noticeable—by us or by others. It doesn't seem like anything has changed. Gradually, others begin to notice. Finally, life becomes routinely boring! Aimlessness gains in attractiveness. But drifting leads to danger as the focus of our faith fades.

The God "who began a good work" in us desires to "perfect" our lives by the presence of His Holy Spirit within us. We need to put motives in our motions. "Why are we doing what we are doing?" is a very vital question. To put it bluntly, "For whose glory are we performing our task?" It doesn't matter what the task is. I have discovered that whether I am preaching a sermon or mowing my lawn, if I am not conscious of the fact that I am a child of God, serving Him, it becomes either a stagnant routine or a parade before the public.

When I ran cross-country races at Hope College, I was happy that it was a team sport, with a team total score. We competed as a team; we celebrated as a team, but more importantly, we represented Hope College as a team. Awareness of our place in the family of God can give a framework for faithfulness.

Whether life is calm or stormy—whatever the day may bring—William C. Martin's hymn remains true:

"Mighty tides about me sweep, perils lurk within the deep, angry clouds o'er shade the day, and the tempest rises high. Still I stand the tempest's shock, for my anchor grips the rock."

The powerful presence of the Holy Spirit gives meaning to the mundane. Jesus washed the disciples feet... forever challenging the Christian to see meaning in every moment, even the most menial!

Sometimes, however, our struggle is with the pressure of priorities. Our calendars can be over-crowded with scheduled events. As we age, our energy is obviously not inexhaustible. New opportunities draw our interest. The multitude of possible engagements make for difficult choices: the things we have always done, new things we haven't done before, the things other people tell us we simply have to try.

Some people seem to accomplish this with ease and tell us, "Just make up your list and put the most important first." But which items on the list are the most important?

Deeper than this is the question, "Most important to whom?" Most important for me? Or most important for God's kingdom? Who controls our calendars? The answer to this question becomes apparent when we ask, "How did this item make my calendar?"

Simply my job? The monetary reward? How much pleasure it promises? The feeling of fulfillment it may produce? Or a deep sense of faithfulness to the Lord of my life?

When we acknowledge the Lordship over our lives—which Jesus rightly deserves and which ought to be the basis for a place in our calendar—the spaces in our calendar can be filled with confidence.

Straightforwardness is an old word with a wealth of meaning. What is the deepest purpose of your life? Where is it all heading? Whom do you really want to please? In every race there is a finish line. And waiting for the runner at that line are those significant people whose evaluations count.

The highest reward is that of the One who speaks: "Well done, good and faithful runner; enter into the joy of your Lord." Recently, a 103 year old shut-in, whom I have been privileged to visit countless times, shared with me in our last visit that she had become so weak that "continuing the race" seemed to be very difficult. Despite her age, she had up to that point been very alert, with an excellent memory and a genuine sense of humor. It seemed to me that the finish line had come into view and she was ready to cross it. The person with her when her time came, described how she raised her arms... reaching upward as she died.

Our race of life may be long or short. The distance does not matter. It is the destination which counts. Our Creator creates; Christ our Savior runs beside us. Our courses are of varying lengths and degrees of difficulty. The indwelling presence of the Holy Spirit empowers us to endure the hills and valleys along the way. The courses laid out for us are made clear as we study the manual for runners called the Bible. Our fellow-Christians are our teammates. We run, not for personal glory, but to honor our Savior.

As we run, we experience troubles, grief, temptations, stormy seasons … but our anchor holds.

What causes drifting?

"Doing what I've always done?"

Yes.

"Catching up with our calendars?"

This, too! But also, being distracted by attractions.

It is easy to be drawn into a dream world. The world is selling us a bill of goods. Its dream avoids reality and ultimately disappoints.

In a multitude of ways, the world is calling us to live out our wildest dreams. Modern media bombards us with suggestions. The draw of dreams always beckons. Protection comes through the anchor-rudder of our life. The anchor holds us to the truth; the rudder guides us by the truth.

What is the solution? Choose the right life goals; then pour all your energy into reaching those goals. Consider all other successes as secondary to knowing Christ and becoming like Him. We may be out of step with the world, but we will be in step with God's plan for our life!

―

Questions:

1. What am I most neglecting?

2. What seems to cause my *drifting*?

3. How can I anchor my life more to God and His Word?

XIII. CHRIST OUR COACH

This series of chapters rightly ends with "Christ Our Coach." Nothing is more important for running the race of life than having Christ our Savior as our Coach—the only one to run the race of life perfectly!

Two books, written by remarkable coaches, John Wooden and Chuck Drnek, have been of tremendous help in my understanding of the challenges of coaching. John Wooden's 88 straight victories and Chuck Drnek's 100 straight dual meet victories are very impressive, but more than that, I deeply appreciate the strong Christian values that permeate their writings.

My personal coaching experience consists of only one season co-coaching a little league baseball team with another dad. My son had come home from the first meeting of his new team only to discover that it did not have a coach! The boys were told that unless some of the dads would step up to coach, there would be no team! Neither of us dads had any experience in coaching baseball. My only qualification was being a dad with five sons. Another dad and I coached the boys and let their baseball abilities stand up to the plate. Believe it or not, we won the championship! I never tried again, and I retired undefeated.

Wooden's book, ***They Call Me Coach***, and Drynek's, ***Lessons from Life*** picture the pattern we seek in making Christ our Coach.

The heart of Drnek's coaching may be summed up with his words, "We tried to teach our athletes lessons that would help them become successful and also become better people in life." Drnek would answer the question, "What is this year's team going to be like?" with, "I don't really know; come back in twenty years and I'll tell you!"

In the Bible, the Christian's relationship to his Coach is pictured as a sheep's relationship to its shepherd. In the 10th chapter of John's gospel, Jesus said, "I am the good shepherd; I know my sheep and my sheep know me... I lay down my life for the sheep."

Every athlete has to endure the imperfections and, sometimes, the impatience of his coach. Running the race of life with Christ as our Coach is the best! For He has perfect knowledge of us as runners, perfect knowledge of the race we are called to run, and patience with us as we run imperfectly,

We are called to be disciples of Christ... not an easy calling. Surely, it wasn't for the first disciples. Often, we picture the disciples as what they became after walking with Him awhile. But their race of life did not begin that way. At the beginning, they were closed-minded, self-centered, self-distrustful, fearful and skeptical—much like our own early efforts.

Under the coaching of Christ, we can become teachable, obedient, self-confident, and faithful as we trust His coaching. But, too often, we begin with thoughts like, *Why would Jesus care about how well I run the race of life? What can be found in my life which is of value to Him?*

The legendary coach Amos Alonzo Stagg often said, "I have worked with boys whom I haven't admired, but I have loved them just the same!" This attitude is infinitely more apparent in the life of Jesus. His love led Him to the cross of Calvary—on our behalf!

One of Coach Stagg's athletes once said to him, "Coach, do you mind if I call you *John*?" During the next few moments he did refer to his coach as *John*. But, suddenly, he stopped and said, "I can't do it! I've tried. But it's going to have to be *Coach*."

If a quality coach deserves the name *Coach*, how shall we speak of our coach? For so many people today, the word Jesus is a swear-word! For others, it is slurred into *Jeez*. Let us resolve to never speak of our Coach other than with awe and reverence!

I love to sing Bill Gaither's song, "There's something about that name... Jesus, Jesus, Jesus, there's just something about that name!"

Far too frequently, today's culture takes in vain a name which should cause us to bow our heads in humility and gratitude.

At the heart of our failures, perhaps, is our tendency to be more concerned about our reputation than our character. But our reputation is merely what others think we are; while our character is what we really are!

In running our race of life we must not mistake activity for achievement. Activity can be merely a surface thing. The achievement of forming Christ-like character is the only worthy goal of our running, for it alone brings honor and glory to where it belongs... to the person of our Savior-Coach!

Team spirit can be defined as, "Eagerness to sacrifice personal glory for the welfare of the group as a whole." It is a kind of togetherness which creates consideration for others.

The ultimate sacrifice was the Son of God, Jesus, who endured the agony of hell in His death on the cross in order that those who accept Him as their personal Savior may run through the finish line directly into His presence and their eternal home!

But winning the race of life requires placing all one's faith in the hands of our Savior-Coach. Without that determination, we run an aimless course, going round and round in circles leading nowhere.

Rejecting the pressures for making points in the judgment of our peers by swerving off course from moral principles is the only path worth pursuing. Our Savior-Coach carefully described and demonstrated the style of race His athletes are to run. To many, it is too straight and too narrow. However, it is the only course which leads to the goal.

Coach Stagg believed there were three things vital to success: conditioning, fundamentals, and working together as a team.

The presence of the living Lord, at work within us, conditions us for the race we are to run. Conditioning is a lifelong challenge for the Christian. For a new Christian, the challenge of a drastic change is great. But, perhaps, the challenge of staying in condition is even greater... all the way to the finish line!

The Bible is the runner's guidebook. It includes the fundamentals for running the race of life. When it is seen merely as a book of rules, it is destructive of running the race. When it is accepted as the necessary guidelines for gratitude to bring glory to the God who sent His Son to do what we could not do—to be qualified for victory—then we run joyfully!

Through my years of ministry (over half a century) I have met many a runner who claimed no need for a team. Being part of a team—a congregation, small group, and etc.—is not simply a good idea, it is essential! Jesus chose a team of twelve. The early Christians huddled together in close relationships with fellow Christians. It is not mine to judge, but the only joyful, victorious runners I have known always chose to run together.

My privilege of being an assistant coach, working with runners struggling to reach the finish line spiritually strong has taught me much about this challenge and its achievement. Every runner runs with their own style, and there is no perfect style! Concerns about physical condition are inevitable. Yet it is the nourishment of the spiritual condition to which we must give greater attention as the finish line nears.

Jesus offers Himself as a model, a mediator, and a mentor. So, how are we to live? As Christ-like as possible. His role, of course, is far different from ours. His role was to be the Messiah. Ours is to believe in the Messiah. But the characteristics of His life form a model for us to follow. He came to be the mediator between His heavenly Father and sinful mankind. His sacrifice makes possible our acceptance by the Father. He mentors us in how to live a thankful life for all God does and has done.

That's why Christians love to sing:

> "How sweet the name of Jesus sounds
>   In a believer's ear!
> It soothes his sorrows, heals his wounds,
>   And drives away his fears.
> It makes the wounded spirit whole
>   And calms the trouble breast.
> Tis nourishment to hungry souls,
>   And to the wary, rest.
> Jesus! My Savior, Shepherd, Friend
>   My prophet, priest, and king!
> My Lord, my Life, my Way, my End,
>   Accept the praise I bring."

("How Sweet the name of Jesus Sounds" by John Newton)

Questions:

1. What do you appreciate most about Christ as your Coach?

2. What do you find most difficult in His challenge?

3. What do you find most exciting?

XIV.   RUNNING HILLS

Life has its ups and downs. Sometimes we feel like we are running uphill; other times we feel more like we are running downhill. Eventually, we reach a stage more adequately described as over the hill!

Runners know that much of our approach to running involves not only shifting gears in our legs, but also shifting gears in our heads. Similarly, when life goes too smoothly we tend to live carelessly. By contrast, it is in our days of difficulty that we need divine insight if we are to grow graciously.

The hills of life must be looked upon as things to be negotiated effectively and economically with as little disruption as possible in our running rhythm.

In all of life's hill experiences we need to surrender the pattern and the practice of life to the God who created us and through Christ redeems us. To achieve such a lifestyle, we need a close relationship with our Coach, the Lord Jesus Christ, who became man to run "the perfect race" and to offer Himself as our Coach in understanding and undertaking our race.

The Christian life isn't a hundred yard dash. It's more like a marathon. It can be a very long race! And long races don't require speed as much as they require grit, determination, and finishing power.

We are more likely to injure ourselves when running downhill in life because of the increased impact on our feet, ankles, knees, and legs. Even coasting can be costly! Some of us handle life's up-hills better than others. And others handle life's downhills better. The strategy and tactics of the Christian life, like the strategy and tactics of the runner, are complex.

Our goal is to negotiate life's race as effectively and

economically as possible and with as little disruption as possible to the rhythm of our lives. Running the race of life well may not add years to our life, but it will add life to our years.

Running the Race of Life

by

Cornelius A. Van Heest

Author, Perfecter of our faith.
Jesus the Son of God,
Help us, we pray, to run our race—
A course the saints have trod.

Remove from us, O Lord, we pray
The hindrances and the sin,
To run with perseverance,
The crown of life to win.

Help us willingly to accept,
The race marked out for us.
Remembering the cross you bore,
Till we your face shall see.

While saints surround us like a cloud,
Throughout our life-long meet,
Help us to cross the finish line,
To fall at your blest feet.

—

Acknowledgements

I want to express my appreciation to my wife, Mary Lou, for her encouragement and support.

In addition, I would like to express my gratitude to my son Wayne for illustrating the cover and to my son Tom for editing the book.

Biography

Cornelius Van Heest was born in Catskill, New York. His father Reverend John Van Heest and mother Lucille raised two sons who became pastors and raised five daughters who married pastors.

Cornelius graduated from Hope College in 1952 and Western Theological Seminary in 1955. He served 55 years in ministry in seven churches as pastor, and eight churches in interim ministry. In addition, he served five churches in senior adult ministry.

In 1954, Cornelius married Mary Lou Richards. They raised five sons and have seven grandchildren. In 2014, they celebrated their 60th Anniversary.

Made in the USA
Lexington, KY
06 July 2018